BEING
Different
THAN
MY FAMILY

Living with
Mosaic Down Syndrome
Chromosome #21

JONATHAN WINCHELL

authorHOUSE

AuthorHouse™
1663 Liberty Drive
Bloomington, IN 47403
www.authorhouse.com
Phone: 833-262-8899

Published by AuthorHouse 12/21/2022

ISBN: 978-1-6655-5187-8 (sc)
ISBN: 978-1-6655-5191-5 (e)

Print information available on the last page.

This book is printed on acid-free paper.

In Loving Memory of

Harry Saul Winchell
1935–2007

Devoted Father, Grandfather and Husband

*A believer in the power of world cinema
to bring people together.*

Dedicated to my Dad, Harry Saul Winchell.

CHAPTER

1

OVERVIEW

How was I raised being born with mosaic down syndrome?

I was afraid of failure when my parents did not prepare me for what my life would be like being born with mosaic down syndrome. What happened to me? I was raised to share how I feel and that includes anything personal with the challenges I went through. I always knew my parents encouraged me to elaborate knowing I was born with mosaic down syndrome. So when I asked my dad about my disability as a teenager if he could correct my mosaic down syndrome. He didn't have an answer right away because he was stunned that I asked him the question. It would have been nice to get some feedback from my dad. My dad did what he could, unfortunately it was a failed research because it was all talk. I just wanted my dad to politely explain about my disability.

My parents took me to specialized classes before kindergarten so I would be prepared for public school for two years. Then after two to three years in public school I then went to a private school because my parents saw that my public school didn't have any specialized classes for my disability. Looking back as a child I wished my parents would put me in a private school instead of a public school. When I did go to a private school for one year, I remember I had a great teacher, unfortunately the students had a lot of emotional issues. So my parents took me out and put me back to finish my remaining years in public school. Looking back It was very tumultuous for me from K-6 being born with mosaic down syndrome. I never embraced my disability when I was younger because my education wasn't easy. I had no specific educator that enhanced my skills in my grammar, reading and writing. I also didn't have anyone to help me with my social skills. It would have been nice to feel good about myself and possibly have good social skills with my peers and share my feelings with my parents.

I did not know that my emotional issues stemmed from my disability in growing up. My brain cells didn't function that well as a child. I eventually did pretty good for myself as I got older. I also didn't embrace my disability because it wasn't talked about in my parents house. I knew later on in life I was high maintenance because I was easily excited and wanting my parents attention. I never got their attention because in looking back they were very matter of fact and they never shared emotional issues; it was only when they were alone.

Looking back on what happened to me in K-6 grade, I didn't like the idea that I was being transferred from a public school to a private school because not only were they both different challenges I felt like I didn't have a choice. I would have preferred to go to a private school with specialized classes. I would have been better off in a private school because there would be smaller classes and the teachers would help me through my disability. I was a teenager when I told my parents I wasn't happy in my public school in my Junior High because they put me in a specialized class so they took me out. It affected me very hard where I couldn't deal with it in my parents house because my parents never felt comfortable talking about emotional issues because they were both matter of fact.

What stages did I go through in being born with mosaic down syndrome?

As a teenager, being born with mosaic down syndrome at home was very hard. I remember as a teenager I needed help on my homework after school so I went home doing an assignment in reading a book on John Steinbeck Of Mice and Men. I tried my best to do it on my own unfortunately I had a reading disability and I was struggling. So I went to my dad because I was frustrated trying to understand what I needed to do. Unfortunately my dad wasn't receptive because he was on the computer doing his research and development as a doctor. I then made a comment to my dad about my problem with my assignment and I said to him no man is an island his response was I am doing the best I can son. From that day forward on as time passed I grew more frustrated and disappointed because with all the hard work my dad has done to help his family it made me feel that he put his work ahead of me. I got to resist my family for giving me the wrong information most of my life. When my dad finished his work he took me out and we had a good time. I do remember the good and bad times in growing up at home being born with mosaic down syndrome.

When did I know I had Mosaic Down Syndrome?

I was in Junior High School where I remember for a short time I took specialized classes in a public school and it affected my mosaic down syndrome. The reason why my parents took me out is because there were students that had emotional issues and I wanted to be treated fairly. I didn't have that many emotional issues in public school, I just went home and expressed my emotions and feelings. In my second and third year of Junior High School there were students that were smarter than me and the classes were harder. It frustrated me knowing my parents did the best they could, unfortunately my upbringing being born with mosaic down syndrome was not talked about. I wished it was discussed so I would have been prepared and asked questions unfortunately that is the way it was.

Where did I go to get help being born with mosaic down syndrome?

I was taken by my parents to see a speech therapist in two places, one in my hometown and the other just ten to fifteen minutes away. It helped me prior to going to school and it prepared me for the short term. I just wished I would have been there longer so I could develop my intellectual and social abilities. As time passed I communicated with my parents to stay longer because I was very motivated to learn and had high expectations for myself.

Why does my family underestimate my mosaic down syndrome?

I proved I can overcome my disability where my parents didn't see that I may have intellectual abilities or even intellectual challenges being born with mosaic down syndrome. They only saw me struggling where in reality I felt they held me back and micromanaged my business life, social life, investing and didn't think I could do things on my own. This was very disappointing to say the least. I felt I was being controlled and being overprotective of me. I overcame my abilities and I am very proud of my accomplishments. I was alone, depressed and I didn't embrace my hardship because it wasn't talked about. When I did things on my own by finding my own job after my dad passed away my family didn't embrace what I can do on my own and it was very bittersweet.

What are my strengths?

My strengths as a young child were that I was very competitive in sports (physically and as a hobby). I had physical stamina where I took tennis lessons and more importantly my parents were good at tennis also. I took public and private lessons from professional tennis players and I went to a tennis camp up in Lake Tahoe. With everything turning out good for me something happened to me that was disappointing as I was competing getting ready to join a junior tennis camp because my counselor saw potential in me and I felt good. So my parents didn't think I was good enough because they didn't think I could handle the stress and they said to me there are kids stronger and better than me. What I understand now is that I didn't know back then that they overprotected, controlled, and held me back because of my mosaic down syndrome.

My other strength is having the ability to read people's feelings, their expressions and facial features by reading between the lines. What that means is I have a high emotional intelligence that measures my reasoning and problem-solving abilities. In my case I use my non verbal abilities such as visual illustrations to get by. I have the ability to embrace hardship no matter what stresses come my way. I like sharing my interests, hobbies such as collecting sports and non sport cards. I also like to share my knowledge of music, movies, broadcasting and sports.

What were my weaknesses?

I used to be delayed in my speech where I didn't speak in complete sentences. I just used words and my speech therapist put them in sentences for me. This was when I had problems in reading and word problems regarding my math. There were also times and moments that my disability took over the best of me. It didn't feel right especially when it wasn't discussed in my parents house where they always looked outside for others to help me. I felt there were too many issues with my mental health, especially being born with mosaic down syndrome as a young child throughout my adulthood. This wasn't a good feeling that I had in growing up. At that matter shouldn't there be trial and error whether as a son or a student at that matter.

Why were my normal cells not talked about and my mosaic down syndrome was?

I learned on my own that my normal cells weren't discussed because my parents were only focused on my cells that had mosaicism. They knew my mosaicism wasn't common so why test my emotional intelligence knowing that my normal cells show less developmental delay than me as a child being born with mosaic down syndrome. I noticed as I got older my normal cells took over my mosaicism. I have good verbal abilities and visual-perceptual skills in paper-and pencil tasks. I also could tell when my parents were frustrated and disappointed in me by their facial expression especially when my mom gave me the evil eye. That is when I got frustrated and disappointed with them and I didn't feel good about myself. Growing up living in my parents house wasn't easy for me because they didn't have a disability and when things were hard for them is when they saw me struggle dealing with my mosaic down syndrome. What was hard about my developmental difficulties was that my parents had to intervene by taking me to see a speech and language therapist because I looked physically different than a regular child who doesn't have a disability. As a young child I never knew the impact of benefiting from additional support in schools when I was younger. Being born with Mosaic Down Syndrome I wish there was someone I could have talked to about what I went through. It probably would have had more of an impact on me.

I would have liked to overcome my mosaic down syndrome on my own. What that would like for me is providing for myself a place that I would call my own business. If I overcome my challenges I would have done good for myself by using instrumental assistance at my disposal; such as acts to perform my work tasks like providing myself with information, making introductions to contacts or offering advice from others. In my thirty years of experience I was never shown how to improve my quality of life at my home and my work with my family. It would have been nice for my dad to show me the ropes of the business instead he showed my younger sister the ropes of the business which I didn't know till my dad passed away.

My dad always told me he would rather do his doctor's duties and responsibilities because he was happy doing that. Unbeknownst to me it took me a while to acknowledge he showed my sister the ropes of the business. I felt hurt. When I did realize what happened I felt motionless and I wished I had taken a bigger role in the business. It hurted me for a long time and then I made a decision on my own to leave the family business. This was way after my dad passed away. When I did move on my family wanted me to stay by holding me back.

They also were holding onto the past in honor of my father. It felt good when I did move on because I did many jobs on my own after thirty years in property management because I wanted to see what the world would be like. The second challenge I tried to overcome was no emotional bonding, socializing with my parents, no joking and not providing space to vent, and my parents not showing an authentic interest in my personal life unfortunately that didn't work out for me. I always felt my mosaic down syndrome was unrecognized especially when it wasn't talked about. That is when it hit me the most.

My third challenge is not being able to connect with my parents because I was high maintenance as a teenager and as a young adult. For example, I always wanted my parents attention and I had emotional issues that were problems that my parents couldn't solve because of my mosaic down syndrome. It was a hard time and very sad to say the least.

I always wanted my parents to be helicopter parents so I can share all the good moments that I had accomplished on my own, not just how difficult it was for me being born with mosaic down syndrome. I looked up to my dad because he was a renaissance man. Unfortunately my parents did not show a close relationship with me meaning the struggles I had. My parents were both stoic through their body language. Both my parents were affectionate towards me, unfortunately my parents didn't talk that much with me, they talked when they were alone. Looking back it was frustrating because I felt overlooked because of my Mosaic Down Syndrome and I didn't feel I was treated fairly, valued, respected and connected as an individual.

I was surprised when I found out later in life that my parents were surprised to learn I had Mosaic Down Syndrome a month after I was born. Their expectations had been that I would be normal, but after they heard from the doctor saying, "He won't read, he won't be able to drive, he won't be able to have kids, he won't have a job," my parents replied, "We will see how far his abilities will go. As I look back, I have accomplished a lot on my own.

CHAPTER

2

HOW MY FAMILY DYNAMIC AFFECTS MY DISABILITY

What makes my Mosaic Down Syndrome hard is that I am going through this alone, since my parents didn't know much about managing my disability; such as my language, speech, and enhancing my social skills. I didn't feel accepted and appreciated through acquiring certain skills I could have. I even remember as a kid we got second hand books from my cousins from my mom's side and then once we got the books because I was too young to read my cousin from my dad's side read to me and my siblings. I wish I had a support system so as I got older I can share with my family what I've been going through. Fortunately as I got older I showed a lot of independence, not just because I was the oldest of four I was mature enough in dealing with my normal chromosomes.

Looking back my parents and my siblings only saw my disability, which caused my family to overprotect me and not recognize my strengths. What I have learned as I got older is that I was happy when I earned my own living, knowing that I was independent from my family. That is when I went out on my own. I felt secure at the moment. Then there was a moment in time where my family thought I wouldn't be able to do things on my own and grow up to make my own decisions. It distracted and frustrated me when they didn't recognize what I could achieve. They held me back and it wasn't a good feeling that I had back in the day.

I have so much to give; such as knowing when to listen, putting others first before I speak and have a genuine interest in others. This all started when I was managing apartments, managing tenants, and getting the best out of people. I learned all of this because I didn't like myself seeing that I was being micromanaged by my parents and my young sister after my dad passed away. I promised myself to be a Macro manager to get the best out of people unfortunately things didn't work out for me. I just moved on knowing my dad always put others first in his industry as a doctor; it just didn't translate to my expectations of him. I love him very much and still miss his presence to this day.

When I was younger being the older son I fought with my siblings changing the TV station so I could watch wrestling from 1977-1983 instead of watching cartoons.

When I did watch cartoons it was from 1968 through 1976. I remembered watching The Banana Splits, Romper Room, Mister Rogers Neighborhood and Sesame Street. This was at that time I memorized the TV Guide. I even remembered all the channels, the name of the TV shows, and the times they played. I found out many years later my grandmother from my mom's side watched Gorgeous George, a wrestler from the 1950's. My family told me wrestling was fake unfortunately my mom never told me that her mother liked wrestling or sports for that matter. I also found out my grandmother loved baseball and I never knew how active my grandmother was. I was also very lucky that my grandmother taught me bowling at a young age because somehow she knew I enjoyed sports. Later on in life I knew I was very comfortable and enthusiastic about the past, being very nostalgic, reminiscing and sharing my enthusiasm because my grandmother and my great-grandparents enjoyed watching wrestling and baseball from the 1930's through the 1950's. As I look back, sports were a major component of my livelihood.

I also remember years later when my parents lived in Rossmoor and I was still with my family business, there was a situation at work where my back was to the wall, and my dad gave me advice that if anyone puts you against the wall, figuratively speaking, use your ace of clubs. I won't ever forget what he said. What that meant to me is that if anyone puts you on the spot, don't let that happen. My dad always made statements instead of discussing the details of what happened to me. My feelings after that happened on one hand things went well at times and other times I got frustrated because my mosaicism took over my regular cells. I didn't want to say anything that would sound off being insensitive, so I took the high ground and respected my parents.

When I first worked for a living in the family business doing accounting for our residential complexes I had no experience because I had to do everything on my own. My dad had expectations that I either would land on my feet or not know how I would handle myself because of my disability. To me it was the latter because I always expressed to him that I want to learn everything from my dad. My dad's response was if you want to talk about business or homework make an appointment. It was many years later after twenty two years being in the family business that was when my dad passed away in 2007 and all my family members said to me you need to show appreciation. In reality those were the expectations from my family that were unsustainable and I was getting mixed emotions from them. I was very high-functioning being born with mosaic down syndrome it just got to the point after my dad passed away my disability wasn't embraced by my family. Then I decided to see a therapist for my mental health and when I asked my mother and siblings to come with me they all said I want to grieve on my own.

What my parents and siblings don't know about my mosaic down syndrome is just because I have struggles that doesn't mean I can't have my own personality, values, and sense of self independent of my parents. My independence was facilitated by my personal growth and it helped my ability to develop my own identity.

It was emotional for me when I saw my parents and siblings succeed while I struggled most of my life being born with mosaic down syndrome. There were times I felt I had to work harder than other people at school and at work because that was what my parents expected from me. So I became my own person. This was at a time where sports were very important to me. Unfortunately my parents did not push my hobbies, interest, skills and talents that I had in sports and to me that is sad. I wished I had a support system so as I got older I can share with my family what I've been going through. It was bittersweet as I got older. I showed a lot of independence, not just because being the oldest of four children, it was because I was very competitive. I didn't know how to deal with my regular chromosomes being normal. Looking back my family only saw my disability which caused them to be overprotective and not recognize my strengths. What I have learned as I got older is that I was happy when I earned my own living. I was also happy that my disability didn't stop me from being independent. Nobody in my family thought that I would be able to do things on my own and grow up to make my own decisions. So after many years of working for a living I got frustrated and I got bothered that my family didn't recognize what I can achieve in the family business. I started working in 1985 at my family business in Real Estate, specifically in property management where I first started doing accounting with hands-on experience such as filed work orders and inputting worker orders into a software system and I closed out work orders.

I became a manager in one of the apartments and the other apartment I was an Assistant Manager. I then documented work orders, communicated information to maintenance personnel. I even had experience with administering the work order process through completion, and interacted with tenants. It was also hard for me to know if my parents were happy or unhappy with me. It would have been nice to hear from my parents on how I would have fit in working with others. I never felt I had a good first impression with my parents working for them or with them because my dad always had to find things to correct. My dad was focused on being a doctor. One of many things that I learned is having an interest in the operations of the family business and to see how things work at home. I didn't have discipline and structure at home. Back in the day I could do anything that I wanted and say fortunately I controlled myself both on a business and personal level because my parents raised me to put others first before your own needs and wants. That did work for me on a professional and personal level because my siblings and I could do anything without having any serious communications and consequences with my parents. Oh, boy and that was how my home and business life was.

What makes my Mosaic Down Syndrome hard is that I am going through this alone, since my parents didn't know how to manage my speech impairment and enhance my social skills. I didn't feel embraced and appreciated through acquiring certain skills I could have done for myself.

My earliest moment in having mosaic down syndrome was when I was having problems at school and couldn't communicate with people my age. I did however communicate with my parents regarding school, unfortunately my parents didn't discuss my classes to see how I was doing or even read to me because they wanted me to function on my own. Living with mosaic down syndrome wasn't discussed. On a positive note, being born with mosaic down syndrome I walked on my own to Baskin Robbins an ice cream parlor in the early 1970's. I got a scoop of ice cream on a cone and I even remember paying fifteen cents. Unfortunately it was twenty five cents and the store owner said to me don't worry. That was my first experience earning money by doing chores in my bedroom. Then as I walked home because I knew where I was going my parents got worried about where I was. I mentioned to my mom at first where I was going and she didn't take me seriously for whatever reason. Who would believe a seven year old child. This was at the time where my parents allowed us to do whatever we wanted with no supervision because my dad was in the bedroom doing research being a doctor that he was. Then my mom was doing chores and we were outside of our patio playing.

I felt being born with my mosaic down syndrome impacted me in every aspect of my life. It was like the clouds were gray and it would last for a lifetime. Nothing was easy for me. The lack of me communicating to my parents was very difficult. I even remember asking my mom why kids my age are making fun of me. Her response was kids made fun of you because you were different and they stayed away from you. My mom also said your siblings were your friends and it was hard for me seeing you upset. As I look back on talking to my mom in asking questions about my childhood it made me realize we only talked about that moment and not discussed my overall struggles being born with mosaic down syndrome. I was hoping my parents would have shared with me what it is like struggling with me being born with mosaic down syndrome. I did realize school was hard and even having friends wasn't even possible. My parents were very matter of fact and they didn't show their emotions with me. To me that is a recipe for disaster to me and boy I acted up in public to get their attention. At that moment it didn't matter to my parents if

I had a disability because they were either embarrassed or didn't know how to deal with me being born with mosaic down syndrome. I think it was both however I digress. It would have been nice to see my family support me instead of putting up with me.

Back in the day my family controlled their emotions so I wouldn't get emotional unfortunately I didn't turn out to be the person my parents wanted me to be because they wanted me to be fully functional. It was very hard for me especially after my dad passed away in October of 2007 because it was a couple days later when I turned forty two. I felt the rug was pulled out of me because I wanted to work with my dad so badly unfortunately fate would come back to bite me.

I remember early moments when I was a child when I did have good moments with my siblings while my parents were working around the house. Unfortunately once my parents knew what we were doing it was quite eventful to say the least. When I was six years old, my sister and brother were on top of our neighbors roof and my parents didn't know where we were. My siblings and I were very creative unfortunately the owner didn't think it was funny and he wasn't happy. So the owner wrote a legal letter to my parents saying your kids are naked on my roof. So my parents walked next door and got us off the roof. In looking back my mom said to me you and your siblings were very close to our neighbors. Suffice to say me and my siblings were very advantageous. Looking back I did things on my own with my siblings. You can say we were not disciplined. After this happened my parents locked us in the house so we couldn't do things on our own devices. However I was very creative and unlocked the latch on the door to go out and play. It was a good moment in the early 70's on the other hand my parents weren't happy. Oy Vey! I lived freely and precariously to say the least

As a teenager in school being born with mosaic down syndrome it was hard because of my reading, word problems with math and not communicating in sentences. Oy, more struggles to come. With struggles I did have strengths thank God. I was good at spelling, memorizing and math. I was awkward socially and I was embarrassed about my disability. I still didn't see the light at the end of the tunnel. I can't overstate enough that I like sharing my interests, hobbies and genuinely interested in others. What stands out to me is how I am different from my family. I like to look at myself as a producer behind the scenes and bring it out to others so they appreciate what I have gone through in being born with Mosaic Down Syndrome. I want people to understand what mosaic down syndrome is and how to talk to their kids who have this disability. I found out on my own as an adult I was unaware of this chromosome anomaly and once I knew what was going on there was a light at the end of the tunnel.

As a parent being born with mosaic down syndrome the proudest moment was on Thursday, August 19, 2021 after dinner as the sunset went down my wife and I with our boys were all sitting on the couch in our TV room silent with no background noise, and we all then cried together sending our youngest son Matthew to college the next day in Worcester, Massachusetts. That is where we heard he got accepted to Worcester Polytechnic Institute. It was an emotional moment for my wife and I. I was proud that my wife and I did a great job in raising our two wonderful boys. Our oldest son Adam lives in Chicago with his girlfriend Julia and he has a job in the technology sector and my wife and I are very proud of both of them. Now, a new era is coming for my wife and I as we explore our new lives without our boys as empty nesters.

CHAPTER

3

Jonathan Winchell Volunteering for Civic & Community Causes

In 2000 to 2001 I was an underwriter for the Lafayette Arts & Science Foundation in Lafayette, Ca in my hometown by volunteering in their office by sending out flyers, collateral materials and filing account payables. This was my first experience in volunteering and I had a great time in getting exposure behind the scenes where I can make a difference in my son's education and helping the Lafayette School District and other businesses where they can bring their services to the forefront like; Art (painting, pictures) Science; (Rube Goldberg); Musicians; (singers and other entertainers to entertain the city of Lafayette) these were the good times. Retailers came out, various businesses were there in supporting the Lafayette Art & Science Foundation aka LPIE (Lafayette Partners In Education). Then from 2002 – 2006 I was a volunteer and on the board for the Lafayette Chamber of Commerce and I helped out for the Lafayette Art & Wine Festival. I helped with setting-up vendor signs and road signs. I worked with the Lafayette Police to control traffic. Many years later I became a CERT with the (Lamorinda Community Emergency Response Team).

I then became a benefactor for the East Bay International Jewish Film Festival from 2007-2010 in sponsoring a film in honor of my dad who passed away in October of 2007. In 2008 I then decided to volunteer and to be on the committee by reviewing movies. I provided sponsors, and I went door to door and used my own money for advertising for the Jewish Film Festival. Unfortunately with all the services I did and being one of the top Sponsors and my mother being the other top sponsor things didn't work out for me. Oy Vey!

I was also a former Benefactor for the Lamorinda Film Entertainment Foundation because I had experience in marketing and sponsoring others and I always enjoyed it. I knew both Efi Lubliner and Jo Alice Canterbury before they started this foundation. We were all on a Film Festival committee together by watching screeners of all different types of movies. I was then introduced by Efi & Jo-Alice to Derek Zemrak who was the operator of the Orinda & Rheem Theatre because Derek Zemrak had brought his California Independent Film Festival from Pleasanton, Ca to the Moraga and Orinda Theatres.

They have always been nice to me and it was a pleasure working with them especially being on a film festival committee all together where we all screened films. Then the most amazing thing happened to me from 2009 to the present. I didn't know it at that time I have always enjoy marketing because I wanted to market the Lamorinda Film Entertainment when my friends Efi and Jo Alice & I were all on a committee they introduced me to Derek Zemrak who was the future operator for both the Orinda Theater & the Rheem Theater he wanted to bring his film festival that he founded and we all welcomed him to the Lamorinda area because Derek had brought his film festival from 1999 I So I have known Derek Zemrak for thirteen years and we literally shared stories about blood, sweat and tears literally and figuratively speaking in the film business. What is amazing I have always looked at things from an Independent Filmmaker and that's how I got my start. I was a gofer behind the scenes.

I was an Executive Producer from 2011 to 2016 for various films that I was in and underwritten films working with an independent film company that produced feature films, and short films. I also found a location for the film that would have been distributed to a major distributor in the film industry unfortunately there were circumstances that were beyond my control. I wasn't happy when that happened. That is when things were literally spiraling out of control and we call that creative control in the entertainment business.

My company Winchell Productions was also the main benefactor for the Rheem Theater in Moraga, Ca. for Film Festivals and Documentaries. I was also on KTVU-TV for sponsoring a documentary for the International Film Showcase.

I have been with the Pleasant Hill Chamber of Commerce from 2015 to current and I am currently an Ambassador. I previously volunteered for many events such as the Pleasant Hill Art & Wine Festival, and my previous company FilmBlogsAreUs was the event benefactor for the Kid Zone. My friend Len Shapiro and I provided advertising for the Chamber of Commerce. I was also a sponsor of Diablo Lanes in 2006 in Concord, Ca. The owner of the bowling League

I sponsored asked me if you would like to be on TV and I said yes it would be an honor. This was the first time being on the Jerry Lewis Telethon at the KTVU-TV studio. That is also where I met Mark Ibanez, a sports reporter.

I am also a Staff Photographer for the Bay Area Radio Hall of Fame and a Photographer for the California Historical Radio Society from 2014 to the present where I am a member of both. I have taken photos of various radio stars that became Broadcast Legends in the radio business. My best moment was when my photo was in the Radio Waves in the San Francisco Chronicle taking a picture of John Mack Flanagan, Dan Ethen, Michael Bennett and Steve Dini in 2007 at the Basque Center in So. San Francisco. I remember when John Mack Flanagan was with KFRC back in the 1970's where his mid-day program followed that of Dr. Donald D Rose. I was a part of that target audience back in the day. I also am very happy to be with The California Historical Radio Society located in Alameda where I also take photos of radios from the early 1920's to 1980's and that also includes early tubes because that is how old radio's were back in the day. What I am also proud of is that I picked up radio stations from far away on my radio the Grundig-750 a shortwave radio from my residence in Lafayette, Ca to Pittsburgh, Pennsylvania and that is in radio terms D'xing by receiving and identifying distant radio or television signals, or making two-way radio contact with distant stations in amateur radio. Then years later I received my FCC License. The history of the California Historical Radio Society was first named as Alameda Central 114 years ago and it was a 1900 Sunset Telephone and Telegraph architectural design, which is a California Mission Revival style.

*Here is Bob Brown, James Gabbert, Gary Gielow and Jonathan Winchell
at the Basque Center in So. San Francisco on December 14, 2008*

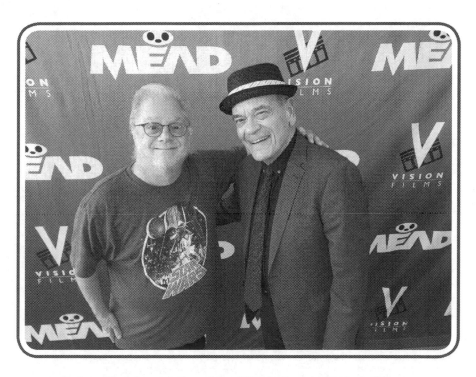

Robert Picardo with Jonathan Winchell at the Orinda Theater
Movie Premiere of MEAD on August 6, 2022.

Here is Ben Fong-Torres with Jonathan Winchell at the
Basque Center in So. San Francisco on June 12, 2019.

Ken Dito with Jonathan Winchell at the Basque Center in So. San Francisco September 10, 2022. This was my first radio call in with Ken Dito on KNBR 680 in the early 90's.

Jonathan Winchell2019 recipient ofthe Legend of the Year!

Jonathan Winchell, Hoyt Smith at the Kofman
Auditorium Center in Alameda, Ca July 2019

Jonathan Winchell a Volunteer for the Pleasant Hill Art,
Wine & Music Festival in October of 2019.

Here is Hank Greenwald with Jonathan Winchell at the Doubletree
Inn on the Berkeley Marina on September 29, 2009.

Gloria Duffy with Jonathan Winchell at the Basque
Center in So. San Francisco on June 12, 2019.

CHAPTER

4

Final Thoughts on my Mosaic Down Syndrome

I was never happy as a teenager and as an adult being born with Mosaic Down Syndrome because I couldn't talk about what I could have achieved; it was only about my challenges that I struggled with. I talked about how hard it was to my parents till I realized as I got older I am unique in a sense that I have normal cells that I could function pretty well. I would say being born with mosaic down syndrome I am smarter than some people who don't have a disability. I say that because I show my verbal abilities and I can demonstrate and visualize my writing skills to express myself. I learned later in life despite my lack of academic and life success I wish I could have used my social skills to embrace my academic hardship. I had little or no guidance from my parents or my teachers, and I never developed the social skills needed to cope with and overcome my challenges. I learned so many skills on my own it's just hard to measure my intelligence.

Had I known about my health concerns as a teenager being born with mosaic down syndrome it would have changed how I would function and my normal cells would have taken over. I found it harder in discussing how things were harder for me, such as slower speech to my parents and to my teachers. That is one reason why my parents didn't talk to me because they saw me struggle. My parents also thought my regular cells weren't quite developed unfortunately they never gave me a chance because things dissipate in time. I would have liked sharing my opportunities, overcoming obstacles and sharing about how I am different. It wasn't about what I needed to know, it would be more about how my life would have changed and my thought process. I would always find a way to welcome new challenges on what is going on with me. It was my parents where they wanted to keep things the way they were. My parents were not versatile because they were concerned at that moment about me all the time. I always felt my parents were overprotective and very controlling. I would have also liked to say to my parents that my mental development was more of an issue than my physical development due to my slower speech. I would say my mosaic down syndrome did not affect my physical development because I was very active physically. I was very good at tennis and I had a great amount of endurance and I could keep up with people my age.

I have noticed for a while that my problem with my Mosaic Down Syndrome is reading and mathematical word problems at school and at home. I wish I could have read a lot more, especially at home with autobiographies which I always enjoyed. I would have liked to read about History of domestic and foreign coins, which has been my hobby from the 1970's to current. I wasn't so good with history which requires memorization of dates and times. As I got older I watched the history channel with my dad. He wanted to watch and I wanted to ask questions. After a while it took me a while to absorb the information.

I was never asked in school by my teachers what do you want to do when you grow up. I never responded because no one ever asked me. Looking back that is how my mosaic down syndrome affected me where I had delayed speech and I stuttered. I would have liked that my parents would help me overcome my delays in my motor skills so they would be able to see my strengths knowing there was a delay in my development and maybe even asked me how I was doing. I enjoyed going to see a speech therapist and I even wanted to stay longer. Instead my parents talked about how worried they were about me when I wasn't around.

I did have the ability to use my fine motor skills to unlock doors, to turn doorknobs, despite my mosaic down syndrome because as the oldest of four I was tall and I had the ability to get into mischief. I knew how to dial a phone, and I even remembered my home number when I was seven years old. My actions spoke louder than words, especially getting into trouble and out of trouble. It was much less about my verbal information back then.

As I got older my motor skills were very challenging because it took me a longer time to complete an assignment, including reading and mathematics. I am more hands on than I am studying to be tested. I never did well. I do remember dissecting a frog because it was a science project and I enjoyed it a lot. If I was taught at an earlier age to make smaller gains in my performance academically or socially I would have enjoyed my life, just like going to college and making friends that would last a lifetime.

I had a lot of challenges being born with mosaic down syndrome. I do remember I couldn't function at times with various subjects as a student. I wanted to learn as much as I can being around my dad side by side so he could teach me about business and even science. I didn't know at that time he kept to himself. He was a great father at times I just wanted to be with him being the oldest of four children. I didn't know the magnitude back then what he had done. I just knew my dad kept alone at work and at home because he was communicating and working together with John Lawrence at the Donner Laboratory in Berkeley, Ca. I would have liked to know what my dad was doing so it would be an interesting conversation. I started communicating when I heard my dad speak. He was well spoken. I learned from my mother after my dad passed away that my dad was almost the head of the Donner Laboratory in Berkeley, Ca by the request of John Lawrence. I was fortunate he took care of his family first and I didn't know that at that time. I started writing my manuscript because I believe both business and family comes first. I didn't know back then what was first or second because I never knew how to separate the two. It was bittersweet for me as time was passing to see my strengths. I knew I was getting better so I helped myself to understand my dad after he passed away by talking to my mom and siblings. I didn't even know that he was an editor in a book with John Lawrence. I would have liked to share my similar interests and communicate with my dad especially when I struggled at home doing homework. I experienced a lot of challenges within my family and now I am excelling in my writing skills and I am very proud of what I am doing.

I do worry at times how long I would live being born with mosaic down syndrome because I have type two diabetes and I do the best I can to lower my blood sugar and at times it saddens me. I do know there may be medical conditions down the road that I may die from surrounding my mosaic down syndrome. I want to embrace my future challenges. It makes me feel humble and I say that because I like sharing my strengths and my weaknesses. I can develop the same medical conditions as those individuals with down syndrome including risks of heart problems, leukemia, digestive problems, mental and emotional problems, cognitive and social delays. I experienced that there is no diagnosis for my mosaic down syndrome because I asked my dad who was a doctor what he could do for me unfortunately when I realized there was no community support and not a sense of an identity for me it was hard to absorb. I am not sure if it got better as time passed. All I know is I need to keep on discussing how I feel and hopefully I will make an impact on the MDS community.

I never expected the best in myself when I was younger because being born with mosaic down syndrome is not who I am, it is what I have. I didn't get attention from my parents, however I did get the love that I needed from my parents. I do feel at times in being a parent and having two wonderful boys I am well adjusted. I also feel at times I am not well adjusted because I wasn't well educated by helping out my boys. I am very happy that my oldest son finished college and graduate school and my younger son will be finishing his second year of college so my wife and I did something right.

I have always felt my emotional and social health were always at risk because of my mosaic down syndrome. What that means to me I didn't get accepted because my mosaic down syndrome wasn't discussed. I definitely had no social connection to talk about my disability. I didn't feel included in every aspect of my family business because of my mosaic down syndrome and I did not feel I had control of my life because I wasn't recognized for my service that I provided for thirty years in property management by being a manager, an assistant manager and in accounting. I feel being an individual doesn't mean leaving the house that I grew up in and doing things on my own. I just wanted my parents to get involved in setting my personal goals such as life skills and my self awareness. I just didn't have that chance because I wasn't prepared. I still remember my Cub Scout motto: Be Prepared! As I got older it's still a work in progress.

I would like to have an advocate by my side in hearing about my stories of being born with mosaic down syndrome by interviewing me. I have a lot of stories that I like to share on how mosaic down syndrome is so underrated. I feel mosaic down syndrome is so underrated because there are so many misunderstandings and not a lot of research or books regarding MDS.

What I now know that I didn't know back then about being born with mosaic down syndrome is that there were no computers or social media talking about my condition or even for me to talk about it. I learned more about my MDS way after my dad had passed away. I have said this before my relationships and work affected me a lot because of my condition. I even remember I didn't tell people about my condition at work. I wanted to keep it separate from my abilities that I had accomplished on my own. I will say when I first started working with my dad and I didn't know it at that time he told the office people my son was born with mosaic down syndrome and most of the people were very supportive of me, unfortunately there was one individual that didn't want me to work because I was born with mosaic down syndrome. After things were settled down my dad found a way to make things right for his family, mostly me because of my MDS so I didn't have to worry about coping with others at work and financial concerns so I didn't have to work on my own. Looking back it was unfortunate I then had to cope with another unruly individual that wanted me to do his work because he/she didn't know how to cope with other people. I was surprised to say the least! I did the best I could to cope with work at times and I did have financial concerns at work and at home. It was regarding accounting that I did and I asked questions at work which I had first hand experience in putting them in a computer system. So I did pretty well for myself at work for many years and at times I enjoyed being around others on a social level.

I didn't get much help from others every step of the way in my work or at home because everyone was doing their own thing. I wished I had help especially being born with mosaic down syndrome so I could have had a better life. I would have liked to have a support group that would assist me with any aspect of living with my MDS, such as eating problems, coping with side effects, talking to people, and managing my work and finances. I would have also liked where I could get a local support group or how to access a counselor. I am happy that I found an online community where I can share my experience and exchange tips with others.

I have a problem with misconceptions about MDS. I didn't want to be born with Mosaic Down Syndrome unfortunately it is what it is. I know it is a disability and for those who don't think it is a disability that bothers me. I have the same mental and physical impairments as a person with down syndrome. I wanted to know as a teenanger how my Mosaic Down Syndrome may be different from teenagers that have standard down syndrome, which made my parents' life difficult. I even questioned if I had MDS or standard down syndrome. I also didn't know the difference between MDS and standard down syndrome especially when there was no discussion on the subject. It was very hard for me and my academics and my social skills were delayed. I would have liked to be tested by doing an Intelligence Quotient test by my parents since they saw me struggle. I now believe when my parents left me alone to my own devices they wanted me to solve my own problems. Fortunately my emotional intelligence far outweighed my intelligence academically. I think that was the difference in my life where my cells have developed and taken over.

I have a better understanding of how my Mosaic Down Syndrome is different from an individual with standard down syndrome. I also know there is not a lot of knowledge or even testing for the development of mosaic down syndrome because there were a lot of misdiagnoses. I know because I asked my dad who was a doctor when I was a teenager to correct my mosaic down syndrome to see what research he can come up with. I found out later there is no research for MDS because I lived my life where my regular cells that didn't have MDS were fine. I had two boys where they did not inherit my disability. I have a good life, I have imperfections with all of that said there is still room for improvement and everyday of my life is a work in progress.

In my experience my emotional intelligence is more important for my success in life than my IQ. I have a natural giftedness in a winning relationship and winning the heart, and doing so is not possible without my emotional intelligence. I may not have a high IQ because of my Mosaic Down Syndrome, however I do have a natural giftedness in my vocation, able to influence others in being reasonable, being versatile and getting the best out of others. I am very effective as a manager, and a natural leader. I have proven that to myself, and at work even though it wasn't recognized by my parents and siblings just like my mosaic down syndrome was when I was younger. My leadership skills have to do with my soft skills: the ability to inspire, persuade, guide, sway and communicate in a way that's heard rather than just being listened to than it is about being the best relative to hard skills. I know living in my parents house their focus was working hard because this is an example of hard skills and not so much of soft skills that I acquired because of my active cells that were functioning and not my MDS cells.

I don't want to take away what my parents did for me by raising me and my siblings, with that said they did not understand my motivations and feelings as a team leader at work and at home, specifically what I did on my own by showing my independence. I started very young as a kid, teenager and as a young adult. I had no supervision however I did let my parents know what was going on with me because of my emotional intelligence. I always understood what triggered my emotions at a very young age because I understood what motivates and demotivates me, evokes feelings of stress or satisfaction, compels me to go above and beyond or not participate at all. I found this especially true with my work, my dad, my younger sister and certain employees from the past. I went out on my own because I wanted to be my own person. It wasn't easy because of the closure. I also wanted to establish my credibility, building my following, and leading with impact. This required my people skills as well as all of my related skills that contributed to my emotional intelligence.

CHAPTER

5

FAMILY PHOTOS

I started going on vacation with my family in 1971 when I was six years old at Disney World. It was a small world after all. I always enjoyed the history of Disney World when I was a child though my adulthood. It is interesting that the ride of It's A Small World was created for the 1964-1965 New York World's Fair. It was Personally overseen by Walt Disney and it was eventually shipped back to Disneyland park, where it opened on May 28, 1966. I kept playing the song in my head. It's such a catchy tune and it reminds me of listening to show tunes in movie theaters. Show tunes were a major venue for popular music before the rock and roll and television era.

When I was young my parents took us to various trips after school was over and it lasted for over three decades before my dad passed away in 2007. It was good times for me and I met various actors along the way. I met Telly Savalas, Michael Landon. I even accidentally called him Michelangelo, Oy Vey! I met Craig T. Nelson, Paul Lynde and Lionel Stander who played Max in Hart to Hart, he was being dressed in womens clothes because he didn't want to be noticed. I knew who he was. I just kept this to myself. These are just a few people that I met along the way.

I will be showing my family photos on the next page when I was younger, and a picture of what I had accomplished and photos with my wife and sons.

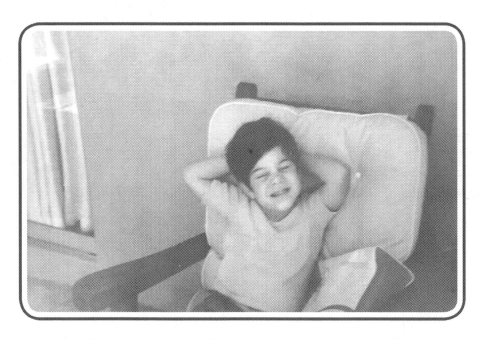

I was five years old in my first house outside on the patio relaxing.

Here is a photo in Chicago of my wife and I visiting
our son Adam and his girlfriend Julia.

Here is my wife and I at the Lincoln Park Zoo in Chicago for a wildlife experience. Established in 1886.

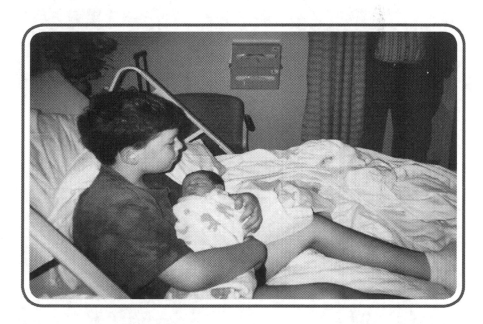

*It was a proud moment for my wife and I having our youngest
son Matthew born with our oldest son Adam holding him.*

This is my youngest son Matthew graduating from Athenian School. What a proud moment!

ACALANES HIGH SCHOOL
Graduation
June 14, 1984

I just received my High School diploma from
Acalanes High School in 1984.

Here is a photo of my wife and I with our son Adam and his
girlfriend Julia at The Signature Room in Chicago.

These are my two boys from (Left to Right) my
younger son Matthew to my older son Adam

My wife Tal and I are at the Botanical Gardens
in Chicago, Illinois - July, 2022

6

Living My Life with Mosaic Down Syndrome

Living my life as a youth it wasn't easy being born with mosaic down syndrome because I was easily overwhelmed with emotions and I acted out when things didn't go well for me. It was hard to separate my feelings with logical decisions because my brain cells that didn't have MDS weren't quite developed. It also didn't help that my parents didn't ask me how I feel because it would have been nice to hear. I also couldn't balance my emotions and reasons when making decisions. In fact my parents made decisions for me which is understandable. I just wished they would discuss this even though it was a difficult time for me as a child and a teenager.

As an adult I had to make adjustments in learning how to deal with being born with mosaic down syndrome. I learned how to embrace my MDS, and be versatile without getting emotional. There are times when something triggers me to get easily excited when things get to me or don't go the way I expect. I don't mind if my family doesn't reply or respond to me right away, just show me the respect of getting back to me even if you don't agree with me. As an adult and making my own decisions I have always replied and responded to others immediately because it is my personality in being outgoing. That is what separates me from my family. I can adapt to changes and in being born with mosaic down syndrome I can articulate my thoughts a lot better than I have done in the past. I couldn't articulate my thoughts in the past because it was difficult.

I never thought as a teenager or an adult if there are things I can do to reduce my risk of MDS progressing, such as exercise, eating a certain type of diet, or taking nutritional supplements. I know not enough is known about my Mosaic Down Syndrome such as adopting healthy behaviors like eating well, getting physical activity, even staying at a healthy weight which has been a struggle in my adult years.

I didn't control my emotions in difficult situations when I was a teenanger because my parents didn't know how to take care of my behavior. I was hoping my parents would have taken me to a Behavioral therapist because they were embarrassed when I acted up in public. I wanted to be the best son possible, I just felt awkward.

As an adult it was easier to control my emotions in difficult situations because I adapted very well and very versatile in challenges that came my way. I still would have liked to go to a Behavioral therapist to help my emotional challenges that can come with Mosaic Down Syndrome. I have always faced physical and mental challenges, but it can also lead to me a full happy life.

My Mosaicism as a child and teenager living with my parents was more challenging because I would have liked for my parents to treat and manage my Mosaic Down Syndrome. I would have liked my parents to have a care provider to monitor my growth, development, and medical conditions. I would have liked my parents to talk to me as a teenager about seeing a medical therapist if I had any conditions depending on my needs.

I would have liked as an adult to go to a Physical therapist to help strengthen my muscles and improve my motor skills. I also would have liked to go to an Occupational therapist to help refine my motor skills and make my daily tasks easier.

Looking back as an adult and in the present I was very fortunate to talk to my friend Len Shapiro about my Mosaic Down Syndrome. He is a good listener, very patient with me, a mentor to me and a great friend. My friend Len and I have similar interests; hockey, baseball, football, minor league baseball and hockey. He and I traveled from different sports stadiums from the SAP Center in San Jose, Ca to the Stockton Arena in Stockton, Ca and he introduced me to several media personnel. I was a videographer for his business in the Bridal Showcase up in Cal-Expo Sacramento, Ca. Len Shapiro and I talked about statistics on various sports. We both were Ambassadors for the Pleasant Hill Chamber where we volunteered and while I assisted with him in his advertising company, I specialized in marketing. What is interesting is that my friend Len and I regularly talk about the pizza business because I didn't know at the time he delivered pizza to my apartments that my family has, how is that for a small world!

My typical day can vary from teaching others how to look at the bright side even when there are hardships all around us.

I have friends that tell me you sound like a Rabbi, a leader and a motivator especially embracing hard times and always keeping a smile. I like teaching others about pop-culture

I also have various hobbies such as learning about the U.S. Coins and Currency and a lot of studying. I first started collecting coins as a hobby in 1977. I am also an ANA member aka American Numismatic Association. I like to relax by watching the History Channel and post what I know on social media sites to keep my family members and friends updated on what is going on in today's technology world and how businesses start.

CHAPTER

7

ABOUT THE AUTHOR - JONATHAN WINCHELL

I am the oldest of four children. I graduated from Acalanes High School in 1984 in Lafayette, Ca. and I took Psychology and Business at Diablo Valley College in Pleasant Hill, Ca. I had few jobs before working in my family business. I worked for KFC in my hometown, I worked at Strings Restaurant in Walnut Creek, Ca and after thirty years in my family business as a Manager, Assistant Manager, Accounting I decided to find an opportunity to get a job in the entertainment industry. I first volunteered and sponsored at various theaters in the East Bay and then I worked at the Veranda Theater in Concord, Ca.

I have been involved in my son's education and sponsoring my hometown community and events. I also have been writing articles in my local newspaper in the San Francisco Chronicle in the 1990's because I have always enjoyed writing articles. I also have been on TV on the Jerry Lewis telethon by sponsoring my local bowling league. I also sponsored the Lamorinda Film & Entertainment Foundation International Film Showcase on TV in my area. I also have been on radio talking to various sportscasters because I have been interested in sports since the mid-70's. I have also been on various board committees in various Film Festivals reviewing films. I also have been on various Chamber Of Commerces Committees in the East Bay.

What most people don't know about my Mosaic Down Syndrome chromosome #21 is that I am very highly functional and my enthusiasm is contagious around others. I believe my disability hasn't stopped me from being creative and having fun at the same time. That is how I overcame my adversity from my upbringing till now. What is missing in my world is creativity and having been used in my daily life. I see my traits are sadly missing and I wish I had these qualities. I always admire creativity and having fun working well together.

Readers may contact Jonathan Winchell via email or social media:

jonbarryzito@gmail.com

www.facebook.com/jonathan.winchell.12

twitter.com/JonathanWinchel

Printed in the United States
by Baker & Taylor Publisher Services